How to Draw the Life and Times of
Warren G. Harding

Lewis K. Parker

The Rosen Publishing Group's
PowerKids Press™
New York

Published in 2006 by The Rosen Publishing Group, Inc.
29 East 21st Street, New York, NY 10010

First Edition

Editor: Melissa Acevedo
Layout Design: Julio A. Gil
Photo Researcher: Amy Feinberg

Illustration Credits: All illustrations by Holly Cefrey.
Photo Credits: pp. 4, 10 (bottom), 22 (bottom), 26 © Corbis; p. 7 © Minnesota Historical
Society/Corbis; pp. 8, 9, 10 (top), 14 (bottom) Ohio Historical Society; pp. 12, 20 ©
Bettmann/Corbis; p. 14 (top) © One Mile Up, Incorporated; p. 16 (top) Courtesy of the Westerville
(Ohio) Public Library and the Ohio Historical Society; p. 16 (bottom) National Archives; p. 18 Marion
County Historical Society; p. 22 (top) U.S. Navy; p. 24 © MPI/Getty Images; p. 28 White House
Historical Association (White House Collection).

Library of Congress Cataloging-in-Publication Data

Parker, Lewis K.
  How to draw the life and times of Warren G. Harding / Lewis K. Parker.— 1st ed.
     p. cm. — (A kid's guide to drawing the presidents of the United States of America)
  Includes index.
  ISBN 1-4042-3005-X (library binding)
  1. Harding, Warren G. (Warren Gamaliel), 1865–1923—Juvenile literature. 2. Presidents—United
States—Biography—Juvenile literature. 3. Drawing—Technique—Juvenile literature. I. Title. II. Series.
  E786.P37 2006
  973.91'4'092—dc22

                                      2005008359

Printed in China

Contents

The Road to the Presidency

Warren G. Harding was the twenty-ninth president of the United States of America. He was born on November 2, 1865, in Corsica, which is present-day Blooming Grove, Ohio. He was the oldest of eight children. Harding's father, George Tryon  Harding, was a farmer and a doctor. Harding's mother, Phoebe, taught him how to read before he was four years old.

When Harding was 10 years old, his family moved to Caledonia, Ohio. Harding did well in school, especially in the subjects of spelling and writing. At age 14, Harding entered Ohio Central College in Iberia, Ohio. He became an editor of the college newspaper. In 1882, while Harding was in his last year of college, his family moved to Marion, Ohio. After graduating from college in 1882, Harding joined his family in Marion and taught for a year there. In 1884, he bought the *Star*, a newspaper in Marion. The citizens of Marion liked what they read in the *Star* and before long, the newspaper became very successful.

Soon Harding began to take an interest in politics. He became a member of the Republican Party, which favored low taxes. In 1898, he ran for the Ohio state senate and won. In 1903, he was elected as the lieutenant governor of Ohio. In 1910, he ran for governor but lost. In 1914, he was elected as a U.S. senator from Ohio and served one term. In 1920, the Republican Party nominated him for president.

You will need the following supplies to draw the life and times of Warren G. Harding:

✓ A sketch pad   ✓ An eraser   ✓ A pencil   ✓ A ruler

These are some of the shapes and drawing terms you need to know:

Horizontal Line	⎯	Squiggly Line	∿
Oval	⬭	Trapezoid	⏢
Rectangle	▭	Triangle	△
Shading	▓	Vertical Line	❘
Slanted Line	╱	Wavy Line	～

The Presidency of Warren Harding

Warren Harding won the 1920 presidential election and was inaugurated on March 4, 1921. His first task was to select the men who would serve on his cabinet. For most of his cabinet, Harding chose some of the smartest men in the nation. He also gave jobs to some of his friends who were dishonest. They caused problems for Harding's administration.

When Harding became president, World War I had just ended and many people were unemployed. Harding set up national programs to hire them. He also lowered taxes, so people had more money. He improved relations with other countries and set up committees that worked to get powerful nations to limit the size of their armies and navies. Harding also supported equal rights for African Americans.

Harding decided to run for reelection. To increase his popularity, he set out on a trip across America to meet the people. However, Harding never completed his trip. On August 2, 1923, President Harding died of a heart attack in San Francisco, California.

While campaigning for the presidency, Warren G. Harding gave many speeches from his home in Marion, Ohio. However, he also traveled to different places in an effort to gain support. This picture, taken in 1920, shows Harding on the campaign trail with other politicians.

THE PIONEER LIMITED

ST. PAUL

7

Warren Harding's Ohio

This house, located in Marion, Ohio, is where Warren G. Harding lived with his wife, Florence, from 1891 to 1921.

Ohio

Map of the United States of America

   Warren Harding's ancestors had come to America from England looking for a better life. His great-great-grandfather had first settled in Pennsylvania and then decided to build a farm in Ohio. Like Harding's great-great-grandfather, thousands of people were drawn to Ohio to build farms. By 1870, 67 years after Ohio became a state, the population had increased to 2,670,000.
   Visitors to Marion, Ohio, can tour the house where President Warren Harding lived with his wife, Florence, from 1891 until 1921. He had the 10-room house built as a wedding gift to her.

Harding used the front porch of the house to give campaign speeches during the 1920 presidential election. The Ohio Historical Society remodeled the Harding home to look similar to the way it did when they lived there. The gas lights, clock, and other objects in the house belonged to the Hardings.

There is also a memorial to Harding in Marion where Harding and his wife are buried. The memorial was built in 1927. Made of white marble, it is 103 feet (31 m) across and 53 feet (16 m) high. The memorial is circular and has 46 columns. The Hardings are buried inside under 17 feet (5 m) of concrete. Their graves are marked by two black-marble stones.

This is the Harding memorial located in Marion, Ohio. The memorial was created to look like a round Greek temple with 10 acres (4 ha) of beautiful landscape surrounding it. It is managed by the Ohio Historical Society.

The Childhood of Warren Harding

Warren Harding was born in the house shown at right in present-day Blooming Grove, Ohio. When Harding was 10, which was about the time the picture of him to the right was taken, his family moved to Caledonia, Ohio. There he attended a one-room school and played in the village band. In 1879, he entered Ohio Central College in Iberia, Ohio. In 1882, his family moved to

Marion, Ohio. When Harding graduated in 1882, he taught school in Marion. He then started working as a reporter for the Marion *Democratic Mirror*.

In 1884, Harding and a friend bought a newspaper in Marion called the *Star*. In 1886, he became the newspaper's owner and editor. Within five years the *Star* became one of Ohio's most successful newspapers. He owned the newspaper until 1923.

1

The house Warren Harding grew up in was built in 1856. It was torn down in 1896. The picture on page 10 was taken with Harding's own camera. To start draw a rectangle. Then add two slanted lines for the fence.

2

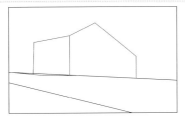

Draw the left side of the house as shown. Add the right side of the house and give it a pointy top. Add a bent line to the top of the left side of the fence beneath the house.

3

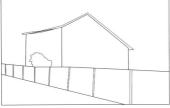

Erase the extra line on the left side of the fence. Add lines to create the edge of the roof. Draw vertical lines along the fence as shown. Draw the bush on the top left side of the fence.

4

Add a line to the left side of the roof to complete the top. Add trim to the roof. Add windows to the house. Draw slanted horizontal lines across the fence.

5

Add more slanted horizontal lines across the fence as shown. Draw a chimney on the roof of the Hardings' house. Add lines to the windows as shown for detail.

6

Erase extra lines. Finish the chimney by adding a curved line to the top. Add more lines to the windows as shown. Add a ragged line below the fence for grass. Add rough horizontal lines across the house. Add lines to the bush.

7

Erase the bottom of the fence that overlaps with the grass. Shade in the spaces between the rails of the fence as shown. Shade in the grass and the house. Excellent work!

Florence Harding

Florence Kling, Warren Harding's wife, was born in 1860. She was the daughter of Amos Kling, the wealthiest businessman in Marion. By 1886, Florence had already been married and divorced. Her father was unhappy with many of her decisions, and as a result, they argued a lot.

Florence moved away and began earning money by teaching piano lessons. When Harding and Florence fell in love and decided to get married, her father opposed the marriage. This did not stop the couple, and they were married on July 8, 1891. After their wedding Florence worked at the *Star* with Harding. Her sharp business sense helped make the newspaper a great success. When Harding decided to enter politics in the 1900s, Florence did her best to help him succeed. When he became president, she traveled everywhere with him. She was with him when he died unexpectedly in 1923.

1 This picture of Florence Harding was taken in 1920. To begin draw a large rectangle. Inside the rectangle draw a big oval as shown. Draw a slanted line connecting the oval to the bottom of the rectangle. Add three more lines as shown for neck, arms, and shoulder guides.

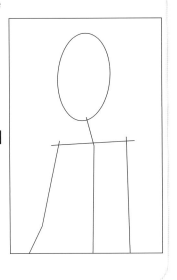

2 Add a curved line to the oval. Add a smaller oval as a guide for her ear. Draw the outline of Florence's body as shown using curved lines and the guides from step 1. Add three straight lines inside the oval as shown for guides to her eyes, nose, and mouth.

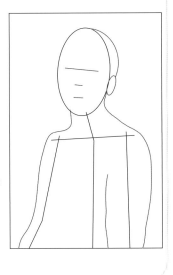

3 Erase the body guides from step 1. Using the guide from step 2, draw ovals for her eyes. Begin her nose as shown. Start drawing her mouth using the guide. Draw her cheeks and jaw. Outline her ear. Start drawing the front of her dress as shown.

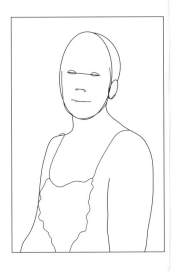

4 Erase extra lines. Draw her hair as shown. Finish drawing her eyes. Draw two small circles near both her eyes. Finish her nose and mouth. Begin drawing the sleeves of her dress. Add shapes to the front of her dress as shown.

5 Erase extra lines. Add squiggly lines to Florence's hair as shown. Add her eyebrows. Add small circles inside her eyes. Using the small circles you drew in step 4, add her glasses. Draw the sleeve of her dress. Add more shapes to the front of her dress.

6 Finish your drawing of Florence Harding with shading. Notice how certain parts of her dress are darker than others. What a beautiful drawing!

Entry into Politics

As the owner of the *Star*, Warren Harding became a well-known businessman in the city of Marion. The people of Marion trusted Harding, and they supported him when he became involved in politics. Harding joined the Republican Party and ran for the Ohio state senate in 1898. The Ohio senate's seal is shown above. He won the election and was

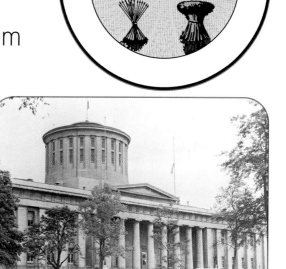

reelected in 1900. In the Ohio senate, which met at the Ohio Statehouse, shown above, Harding was known for settling arguments among opposing sides. Around this time he met Harry M. Daugherty, a lawyer and politician. In 1903, Harding decided to run for lieutenant governor. Daugherty helped Harding get elected by running his campaign. After two years as lieutenant governor, Harding decided to return to the *Star*. In 1910, he ran for governor of Ohio but lost.

1

This seal is used by the Ohio senate. Begin by drawing two large circles. Draw a smaller circle inside as shown.

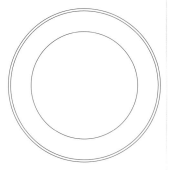

2

Add two bumpy lines inside the smaller circle for the river. Add a squiggly line above the two bumpy lines for the mountains. Draw an *X* in the left side of the smaller circle as shown. Draw the shape on the right side of the smaller circle as shown.

3

Write the word "THE." Inside the smaller circle, draw two curved lines over the mountains for the Sun. Add a pointed mountaintop. Add a squiggly line to the river. Add lines to the *X*. Add detail to the other shape. This will be the bale of hay.

4

Write the word "OHIO." Add more squiggly lines to the river as shown. Add dots to the top line of the sun. Draw shapes around the Sun. These will be the Sun's rays. Draw the bottom of the bale. Add the tops and bottoms of arrows to the lines from step 3.

5

Erase the line you drew the dots on in step 4 so that only the dots remain. Erase other extra lines. Write the word "SENATE." Add lines to the mountains. Draw shadows for the arrows and the bale. Add detail to the top of the bale.

6

Finish your drawing by shading. It may help to look at the picture of the seal on page 14 to shade your drawing properly. Great job!

Becoming a U.S. Senator

After losing the election for governor, Warren Harding got into the U.S. Senate in 1914 with Daugherty's help. In the Senate Harding was in favor of a high tariff. He also supported an organization called the Anti-Saloon League that wanted to make liquor illegal. They used posters like the one above to spread their message. They were able to get Congress to pass the Eighteenth Amendment, shown in the bottom picture. This amendment made it against the law to make or drink liquor.

In 1917, the United States entered World War I. When the war ended in 1918, the treaty that was drawn up called for the creation of the League of Nations. Harding and most other Republicans were against America joining the league. Harding thought the United States would be drawn into more wars.

1

To begin drawing the woman from the poster on page 16, start with an oval head guide. Add a line extending from the oval as shown.

2

Add a curved line to the head. Draw the shape of her body. It may help to look at the poster while drawing the body. Add lines for arm guides. Add ovals for hand guides.

3

Erase the bent line from step 1. Add guides for her eyes, mouth, and nose. Add her hat. Use a curved line to add her cheeks and jaw. Add her right arm and the top of her dress. Draw her feet.

4

Erase extra lines. Add her eyes, mouth, and nose. Add an eyebrow and make her face look angry. Draw her left arm. Add her hair. Draw her neck. Draw the rest of her dress. Start her shoes.

5

Erase extra lines. Add another eyebrow. Draw a line on her chin. Add little circles to the inside of her eyes. Start drawing fingers on both hands. Add lines for folds on her dress as shown. Finish drawing her shoes. Add her toes.

6

Finish drawing her hands. Add a line to her hat as shown. Add stars to the top of her dress as shown. Add stripes to the bottom of her dress as shown.

7

Erase the hand guides and any other extra lines. Finish your drawing by shading. Look at the poster on page 16 for help on how to shade in your picture. Great work!

The Presidential Election of 1920

In 1919, Harry Daugherty and Warren Harding started planning how to get Harding elected president. They felt certain that a Republican 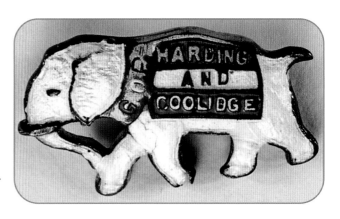 candidate would win because voters were unhappy with the current Democratic president. In a May 1920 speech, Harding called for a "return to normalcy." This meant that Americans should return to the peace and success they enjoyed before World War I. Harding won the Republican Party nomination and began campaigning using buttons like the one shown above and the slogan "Return to Normalcy." Harding, like other Republican candidates before him, gave speeches from his front porch in Marion, Ohio. About 600,000 people came to Marion to listen to him.

Election Day in 1920 was Harding's fifty-fifth birthday. This was the first election in which women were allowed to vote. Harding won the election. He was the first newspaper editor to be elected president.

1

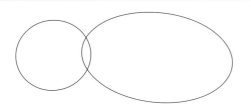

This pin of an elephant, the Republican Party sign, was used in the 1920 presidential campaign. Begin by drawing a large oval. This will be the guide for the elephant's body. Draw a large circle for the head.

2

Draw the elephant's trunk. Add the upper body line, which connects the circle to the oval. Draw the elephant's tail as shown. Draw lines for the legs as shown.

3

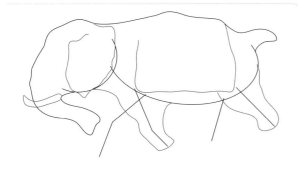

Erase the parts of the guide that go through the upper body lines from step 2. Draw two of the elephant's legs as shown. Add the left ear and tusk. Draw the elephant's blanket.

4

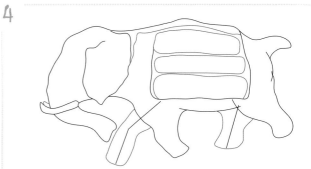

Erase any extra lines. Add the elephant's other tusk. Draw the elephant's other two legs. Draw the shapes on the blanket. Add the line above the blanket as shown.

5

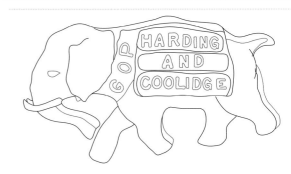

Erase extra lines. Add the eye. Add lines along the elephant's trunk and legs. Add the tip of the other ear as shown. Finish the tail with a line. Write "GOP," which stands for Grand Old Party, along the elephant's neck. Write "HARDING AND COOLIDGE" on the blanket.

6

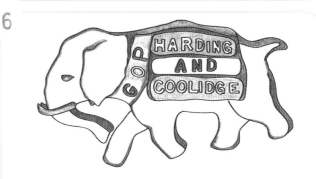

Erase the last of the guides. Finish your drawing by shading in the elephant's eye and the lines you added in step 5. Also shade in the words and shapes on the blanket as shown. Good job!

Harding's First Years as President

On March 4, 1921, Warren Harding was sworn in as the twenty-ninth president of the United States. Harding was the first president to ride to his

inauguration in a car, as shown above.

In his first year, Harding was a hardworking president. He was at his office every day by eight o'clock in the morning and did not leave until after midnight. Harding also made sure that he met with anyone who had an issue that needed his attention. When he was not meeting with officials, he was writing reports, letters, and speeches. Many of his friends worried that he would make himself ill by working so hard because he had suffered from high blood pressure for years. However, Harding did take time off to relax, go to baseball games, and play cards. At least twice a week, Harding and his friends would play cards on the second floor of the White House. Famous people, like baseball player Babe Ruth, often visited the White House.

1

To begin drawing the car in which President Warren Harding rode to his inauguration in 1921, draw a long, slanted rectangle. Draw the shape on the right for the front of the car.

2

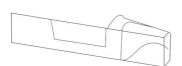

Draw the hood of the car as shown. Start drawing the left bumper on the front of the car. Begin drawing the door.

3

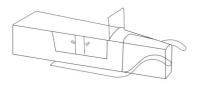

Finish drawing the bumper. Draw the other bumper. Add the windshield to the front of the car as shown. Add lines and handles to the car door. Add the other side of the car as shown using two lines.

4

Erase any extra lines. Draw the car's front tire as shown. Draw the shapes on the sides of the hood. Start drawing the person in the car as shown. Draw the shapes on the back of the car as shown. Add the shape by the door.

5

Erase extra lines. Add the back and front tires. Add spokes to the left front tire and a line to the wheel's center. Draw shapes. Add another person. Add sleeves and a ring for a hat to the first person. Draw a line on the back of the car.

6

Erase extra lines. Draw the center of the back tire and add spokes. Add shapes to the front of the car. Finish drawing the hat on the person from step 4. Add more people. Add a sleeve and ring for a hat to the person from step 5.

7

Erase extra lines. Finish drawing the back of the car as shown. Add a line to the bumper and a line to the front tire as shown. Finish drawing the people in the car and their hats.

8

Erase any extra lines. Finish your drawing with shading. Well done!

Presidential Decisions

As president, Warren Harding carried out many of his campaign promises. He supported lower taxes for companies so that they could make more money. He hoped they would use the extra money to build more factories and hire more people. In 1921, Harding signed a law that limited immigration into America because people feared that immigrants would take the few available jobs.

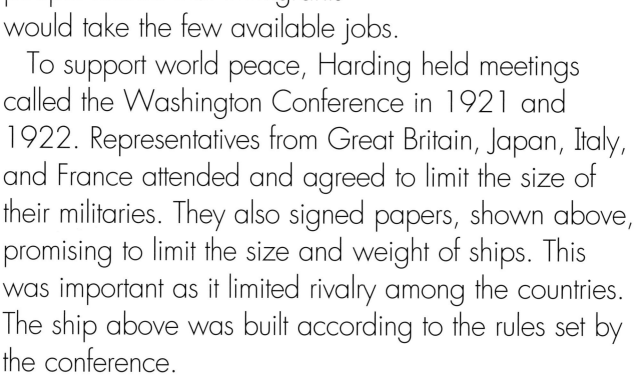

To support world peace, Harding held meetings called the Washington Conference in 1921 and 1922. Representatives from Great Britain, Japan, Italy, and France attended and agreed to limit the size of their militaries. They also signed papers, shown above, promising to limit the size and weight of ships. This was important as it limited rivalry among the countries. The ship above was built according to the rules set by the conference.

This naval ship was completed in 1923, after the treaty had been signed. Begin the ship by drawing a curvy line. Then draw the basic shape of the boat as shown on top of the line you just drew.

2

Draw the boat's windows as shown using dots. Add the lines and shapes to the top of the boat as shown. Add a small line to the front of the body of the boat as shown.

3

Add more windows to the boat as shown. Add lines to the small line on the front of the boat you added in step 2. Add shapes and lines to the top of the boat as shown. Start drawing the boat's guns at the back of the boat.

4

Erase extra lines. Draw a flag at the back of the boat. Start drawing more guns. Add tops to the guns from step 3. Draw two boat shapes at the base of the post. Draw more shapes on the deck. Add small posts to the front of the boat.

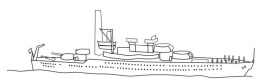

Erase extra lines. Draw more small posts in the front of the boat. Start to add the barrels to the guns. Add the shape next to the gun. Add a tower. Draw the other shapes on the boat as shown.

6

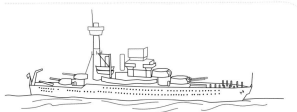

Erase extra lines. Add the shapes and detail lines to the tower. Draw more barrels for the guns. Draw more shapes on the deck as shown. Add squiggly lines in the water.

7

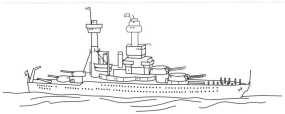

Erase extra lines. Draw the rest of the shapes on the deck as shown. Add dots to the shapes for windows. Draw the rest of the barrels for the guns. Add lines to the boat for detail as shown.

8

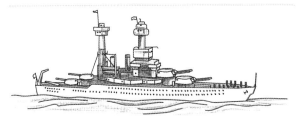

Finish your boat by shading with your pencil. Notice how some parts of the boat are darker than others. You are done! What a great job!

Scandals in the White House

Warren Harding was honest, but most members of his administration were not. They caused several scandals that hurt his reputation. One scandal involved Charles Forbes,

Harding's friend who was in charge of the Veterans Bureau. In February 1923, Harding discovered that Forbes had been secretly selling supplies from veterans' hospitals. Forbes had kept the money he made, which was about $200 million. Harding asked Forbes to resign because he did not want to turn him in.

The Teapot Dome scandal, shown in the cartoon above, involved a place in Wyoming called Teapot Dome. Oil had been discovered in this area and was set aside for the U.S. Navy. Harding gave his friend Albert Fall, the secretary of the interior, control of the land. Fall rented it to large oil companies without the government's knowledge, and he was paid about $300,000. Fall was sent to prison in 1931.

1

The political cartoon on page 24 about the Teapot Dome scandal was drawn by Clifford K. Berryman in 1924. To start the roller in the cartoon, draw the shape above.

2

Add the words "OIL SCANDAL" as shown to the front of the roller. Add an oval to the right side of the roller. Draw a curved shape at the top of the roller. This shape will be the teapot's spout.

3

Draw the shape of the teapot and the lid using curved lines. Draw the opening of the spout using a curved line. Draw an oval shape on the side of the roller as shown. Add spikes to the roller.

4

Erase extra lines. Add lines inside the oval you drew in step 2. These lines should connect to the small oval shape from step 3. Draw small ovals along the side of the oval. Add a curved line along the bottom of the lid. Add a handle and a top to the lid as shown.

5

Finish your drawing with shading. While shading keep in mind that the bottom of the roller is darker than the top. You are done! Excellent work!

The Death of a President

The problems in Warren Harding's administration troubled him. "I have no trouble with my enemies," he had said. "But my friends, they're the ones that keep me walking the floor nights."

Many people were starting to become aware of the scandals in Harding's administration. To increase his popularity, Harding and his wife set out on a trip across America to talk with the people. The trip started in June 1923, and it was supposed to take seven weeks. On July 27, 1923, Harding became ill while giving a speech in Seattle, Washington. He was rushed by train to San Francisco, California, so doctors could take a closer look at him and figure out what was wrong. Doctors discovered that Harding had heart trouble. On August 2, President Warren Harding died at the Palace Hotel in San Francisco, California. A special train, shown above, carried Harding's body across the country to Washington, D.C.

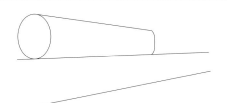

The picture that appears on page 26 of President Harding's funeral train was taken in 1923. Start by drawing two slanted lines. Draw an oval on top of the first line. Draw the long shape behind the oval as shown.

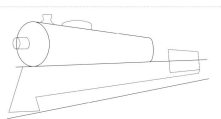

2

Add the shape to the oval from step 1 as shown. Add the shapes to the top of the long shape from step 1. Add the slanted rectangle and connect it to the top line using straight lines as shown.

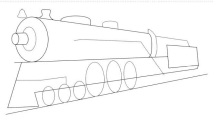

Erase extra lines. Add a curved line around the shape you drew in step 2. Add a bell shape to the right side of the front of the train. Add a curved line to the top of the train. Add lines and circles to the rest of the train as shown.

Add a line to the bottom of the bell and then connect it to the train. Add shapes to the front as shown. Add lines and shapes to the body as shown. Add shapes to the wheels and the bottom of the train as shown.

Erase extra lines. Add shapes that look like hanging sheets. Add lines to the sheet in front. Add new wheels and a curved line to connect them. Add shapes to the front of the train. Add new shapes to the body of the train as shown.

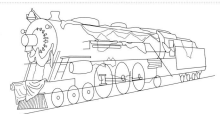

Erase extra lines. Draw lines on the grille in front. Draw more hanging sheets and add lines to them. Add more shapes to the front. Add shapes around the wheels and body of the train. Add lines to the shape near the wheels.

Erase any extra lines. Add lines to the sheet shapes. Add more shapes to the body of the train, including around the wheels.

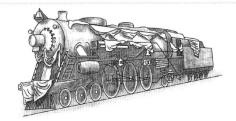

Erase all extra lines. Finish your drawing with shading. Be sure to shade in the bottom of the train darker than the top. Good work!

Remembering Warren Harding

People throughout the nation were stunned when they heard about the death of President Warren Harding. Millions of Americans lined up along the tracks to watch his funeral train as it went by. The president was later taken to Marion, Ohio, for burial.

Throughout his life, Harding risked his political career by taking some bold steps. He supported equal rights for African Americans. At a time when women's suffrage was not legal, he was a supporter of voting rights for women. Harding also created the national budget. For the first time, the president could control government spending. He also worked hard to have a law passed to provide money for the building of highways. These are the things for which President Warren Harding should be remembered. If he had lived, perhaps he might have carried out his promise to bring success and peace back to America.

1 To draw the picture of President Warren Harding on page 28, start with a large rectangle. Draw an oval for the face guide. Draw lines for the neck, shoulders, body, and arms. Draw an oval for his left hand. Draw part of an oval for his right hand.

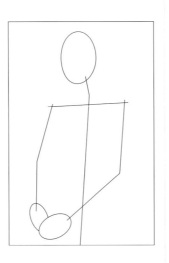

2 Add a curved line to the oval head guide for the side of Harding's head. Draw an oval for the ear guide. Draw guides for his eyes, nose, and mouth. Use curved lines to draw an outline of his body and arms.

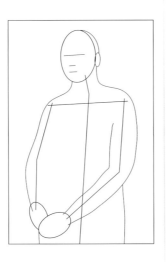

3 Erase the straight guidelines from step 1. Draw ovals for Harding's eyes. Using the guidelines from step 2, draw his nose and mouth. Draw Harding's cheek and jaw using a curved line. Begin drawing his ear. Draw his shirt collar and jacket sleeve as shown.

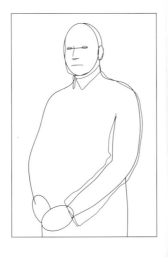

4 Erase extra lines. Add a line to his ear. Finish Harding's mouth. Add circles in his eyes. Add his eyebrows. Add a line near his nose. Draw his hair. Begin drawing his hands as shown. Draw his other sleeve. Draw his tie. Add a line to shape his lower back.

5 Erase extra lines. Draw in his jacket. Start with the collar and finish the jacket by adding lines as shown. Finish drawing both his hands. Add a ring to his left hand. Add lines to his face and ear as shown.

6 Erase the hand guide. Finish your drawing of President Harding by shading. Be sure to shade in his jacket so that it is the darkest part of the picture. Well done!

Timeline

1865   Warren Harding is born on November 2, in Corsica, which is present-day Blooming Grove, Ohio.

1875   The Harding family moves to Caledonia, Ohio. His father works as a doctor.

1879   Warren Harding enters Ohio Central College in Iberia, Ohio.

1882   Harding's family moves to Marion.
He graduates from college.
Harding works as a teacher.

1884   Harding buys the *Star*, a weekly newspaper.

1886   Warren Harding becomes the sole owner and editor of the *Star*.

1891   Florence Kling and Warren Harding marry on July 8.

1898   Harding is elected as an Ohio state senator.

1903   Warren Harding is elected as the lieutenant governor of Ohio.

1910   Harding loses the election for governor of Ohio.

1914   After being elected as a U.S. senator, Harding moves to Washington, D.C.

1917   The United States enters World War I.

1919   Harding's votes in favor of women's suffrage.
Harding also declares that he is against the United States joining the League of Nations.

1920   Harding makes his famous "return to normalcy" speech in May.
Harding is elected president of the United States.

1921   Warren Harding forms his cabinet. He gives positions to many of his friends.
Harding creates the Bureau of the Budget.
He helps set up the Washington Conference.

1923   Forbes is accused of stealing from the Veterans Bureau.
On June 20, the Hardings start on their trip across the United States.
On July 23, Harding becomes the first U.S. president to visit Alaska.
On July 27, Harding becomes sick.
On August 2, President Harding dies.

Glossary

administration (ad-mih-nuh-STRAY-shun) A group of people in charge of something.

ancestors (AN-ses-terz) Relatives who lived long ago.

budget (BUH-jit) A plan to spend a certain amount of money in a period of time.

cabinet (KAB-nit) A group of people who advise important government officials.

campaign (kam-PAYN) A plan to get a certain result, such as to win an election.

candidate (KAN-dih-dayt) A person who runs in an election.

committees (kuh-MIH-teez) Groups of people directed to oversee or consider a matter.

immigration (ih-muh-GRAY-shun) When people move to a new country from another.

inaugurated (ih-NAW-gyuh-rayt-ed) Sworn in as a government official.

involved (in-VOLVD) Kept busy by something.

lawyer (LOY-er) One who gives advice about the law and speaks for people in court.

League of Nations (LEEG UV NAY-shunz) An organization created from the treaty that ended World War I. It was made up of different nations that agreed to go to war if any of the other nations in the League were harmed.

liquor (LIH-kur) A drink that has alcohol in it.

nominated (NAH-muh-nayt-ed) Suggested that someone or something should be given an award or a position.

reputation (reh-pyoo-TAY-shun) The ideas people have about another person, an animal, or an object.

resign (rih-ZYN) To step down from a position.

saloon (suh-LOON) A place for eating, drinking, and playing games. Saloons often rented rooms and held poker games for guests.

scandals (SKAN-dulz) Conduct that people find shocking and bad.

slogan (SLOH-gin) A phrase used in politics or advertising to sell an idea or a goal.

suffrage (SUH-frij) The right of voting.

tariff (TER-uf) A tax put on goods brought in from other countries.

unemployed (un-em-PLOYD) Without a job.

veterans (VEH-tuh-runz) Having to do with people who have fought in a war.

World War I (WURLD WOR WUN) The war fought from 1914 to 1918.

Index

Web Sites

Due to the changing nature of Internet links, PowerKids Press has developed an online list of Web sites related to the subject of this book. This site is updated regularly. Please use this link to access the list:
www.powerkidslinks.com/kgdpusa/harding/